# Santa Fe
# After Dark

An Illustrated Guide
by Bob Eggers

SUNSTONE
PRESS

SANTA FE

A special thanks to Eric Jacobson
who is responsible for the book's layout
and to my friend Suellen Rubinstein
for her encouragement and editing help.

FIRST EDITION
1   3   5   7   9   10   8   6   4   2
Library of Congress Cataloging-in-Publication Data:

Eggers, Bob, 1932-
    Santa Fe after dark : an illustrated guide / by Bob Eggers.
        p. cm.
    Includes index.
    ISBN 0-86534-429-9 (pbk.)
    1. Santa Fe (N.M.)—Guidebooks. 2. Santa Fe (N.M.)—Pictorial works.
    I. Title.
    F804.S23E36 2004
    917.89'560454—dc22

                                            2004007179

Published in

SUNSTONE PRESS / Post Office Box 239 / Santa Fe, NM 87504-2321 / USA
(505) 988-4418 / orders only (800) 243-5644 / FAX (505) 988-1025
www.sunstonepress.com

For Patricia, Genesee and Riley

# CONTENTS

# INTRODUCTION

Good times do roll after dark in our little town. You just have to know where the rolling takes place.

The following pages provide a smorgasbord of nighttime activities and sites from saloons to the opera.

It is wise to check ahead before stepping out for the evening, since the destination that strikes your fancy may have changed it's program, schedule, location or be no longer with us. The local press provides night-by-night, up-to-date information.

The *Santa Fe Reporter* comes out on Wednesday and features the weekly calendar of events in their "Culture" section. *Pasatiempo, The Santa Fe New Mexican's* weekly entertainment guide, is published on Friday and has all the scoop in the "Moving Images" and "Comings and Goings" segments. *Albuquerque Journal North* has details and highlights in the Friday "Venue" section.

Radio is also a good source for information in our community: KSFR (90.7), NPR/KUNM FM (89.9), KHFM (95.5) and KBAC (98.1).

The Bars, Clubs and Lounges chapter
is limited to those sites that either
provide entertainment (music, dance),
a theme (sports bars, casinos) or
other special features.

# BARS, CLUBS AND LOUNGES

# ATOMIC GRILL

115 EAST WATER STREET
820-2866

It's the wee small hours of the morning. The party's over, the bars are closed, you're hungry, you're thirsty, and you're not yet ready to call it quits. What's a person to do?

Not to worry. The answer is downtown on Water Street. The Atomic Grill is a lively hangout with good music, good food and it keeps on rolling 'til 3:00 AM (midnight on Sundays.)

The place really hops in the summer when the outdoor patio is brimming with night owls who are busy people-watching and enjoying music performed by local artists.

The menu includes breakfast, wood oven pizzas, burgers, veggie delights, pastas, ribs and homemade deserts. There's a wine list and 80 beers to choose from.

Bar closes 10:30 PM. Doors close 3 AM. Time to go home.

# BACK ROAD PIZZA

1807 SECOND STREET,
Building #1 (Across from
the Second Street Brewery)
955-9055

Some talented young women have opened a new eatery/hangout in the popular Second Street neighborhood.

The ground floor of this warehouse-like structure is where you will find an open kitchen, performance space and an adjacent patio under the stars.

The upstairs has a couple of pool tables, comfy couches, an outdoor patio and a nice view of the activities downstairs.

Entertainment featuring live music, open mic, etc., happens almost every night.

The real attraction comes from the kitchen. Skillful chefs with ingredients purchased from the local markets produce wholesome and scrumptious pizzas. Add hot subs, calzones and crispy salads to the mix, and you have ample reason to make the short trip from downtown.

Yes, wine and beer are on the bill of fare.

Open seven nights a week until 11 PM or midnight, depending on the crowd.

# BAR B

331 SANDOVAL STREET
982-8999

Adjacent to the clamorous Paramount nightclub, the ever-mellow Bar B is an intimate cabaret with a mix of low light table lamps, art deco chandeliers, flocked wallpaper and faux zebra and leopard-skin chairs.

The bar is well known for it's tasty martinis. The small stage features folk, soul and jazz, with occasional readings, comedy acts, open mic and karaoke. Pizza, sandwiches, Philly steak, subs and salads are available just down the hall between Bar B and the Paramount.

The bar closes at 2 AM. Take-out food 'till 2:30 AM.

# BLUE CORN CAFÉ & BREWERY

PLAZA MERCADO
133 WEST WATER STREET
984-1800

4056 CERRILLOS ROAD
(across from Villa Linda Mall)
438-1800

There are two Blue Corn Cafés. The one in town is a small version of the sizeable sports bar/brewery/eatery on Cerrillos Road across from the Villa Linda Mall. Both noisy hangouts have full bars serving numerous drafts, homemade micro beers, margaritas, wines, etc.

Both cafés serve appetizers such as chicken wings, nachos, green chile stew, in addition to burgers, salads and a full New Mexican menu.

Serious sports fans will probably choose the three giant TV screens on Cerrillos over downtown's two TVs over the bar.

Close at 11 PM Friday and Saturday, 10 PM Sunday through Thursday.

# BULL RING STEAK- HOUSE

150 WASHINGTON AVENUE
983-3328

The Bull Ring Steakhouse is a Santa Fe institution with a rich tradition. Since the doors opened in 1971, this establishment has been the favorite gathering place for state and local politicians who require that their drinks be stiff and their beef be prime.

The pub atmosphere is masculine with an oaken bar and brass rail, dark green paneled walls and clouds of cigar smoke.

Hungry? You can choose from the main menu with the famous dry aged, corn fed U.S. prime steak from Chicago or the bar menu, which includes a delicious blackened prime sandwich, the Bull hamburger, coconut shrimp, and seared tuna.

The kitchen closes at 10 PM. The bartender and pub staff hang in until 11 to 11:30 PM.

THE BULL RING · A PRIME STEAK HOUSE

# BUMBLE BEE'S BAJA GRILL

301 JEFFERSON
820-2862

Bumble Bee's is a happy place. It's bright, it's colorful and everybody seems to be having a good time.

The kitchen's motto is "Fresh is Good," so you'll be treated to "Healthy" Mexican food with daily offerings of tacos, burritos, rotisserie chicken, etc., plus daily specials.

Bumble Bee's also offers both beer and wine.

Music? If you drop by on Saturday and Monday evenings, you will be treated to the mellow sounds of live jazz.

Weekday closing hour is 9 PM. Saturday it's 10 PM. On Sunday it's 8 PM.

PS: It's inexpensive. ¡Olé!

# CAFÉ OASIS

526 GALISTEO STREET
983-9599

~The Mushroom

If you missed the '60s, it's not too late. It's here. The laid back ambience of this old Santa Fe residence was created by a San Francisco transplant who found the City Different "unhip and uptight with no Bohemian magic."

Musicians drop in to play the blues, jazz, folk and flamenco in the "Social Room." But you might want to hang your hat in the "Tahiti Lounge," "Renaissance Room," "Womb Room" or "Mushroom."

Plus, there's a large exotic outdoor patio offering the makings of an evening of infinite possibilities.

The menu includes breakfast at all times, "super hero" gyros, soups, salads and vegetarian dishes, along with beer, wine and margaritas. The kitchen stays open until midnight.

It's a happening 365 nights a year 'til midnight weekdays, 2 AM weekends.

The local press has voted this two-story establishment Santa Fe's "Best Billiard Room" and one of the "Best Sports Bars" in town.

# CATAMOUNT BAR & GRILL

125 WATER STREET
988-7222

Downstairs, the young and restless dine casually and enjoy two TVs, a full bar, and crowd the dance floor when there's live music on weekends.

Upstairs, a large and inviting space features six nine-foot regulation billiard tables, another full bar, three TVs, a balcony overlooking Water Street and the same light-to-hearty offerings as the menu downstairs.

The bill of fare offers appetizers, salads, pastas, burgers and Southwestern dishes until midnight, 11:30 on Sundays.

The bars close at 2 AM, midnight on Sundays.

# CHEEKS

2841 CERRILLOS ROAD
473-5259

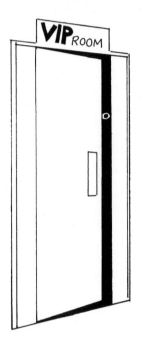

"Harmless visual stimuli" proclaims the sign adjacent to Santa Fe's one and only topless bar.

Male customers are the harmless ones as they hold onto their drinks, sit tight and let the young ladies provide the "visual stimuli." The atmosphere is friendly and upbeat with all the goings-on that make a strip joint a strip joint.

There's even a VIP room, a semi-private retreat furnished with cushy couches where a fella can lounge in solid comfort as he maintains his harmless demeanor.

The front side of the building has had a recent facelift, and that's a good thing, since Cheeks' façade was an uninviting visual for a long time. But who cares, once inside, there's plenty of pulchritude to thoroughly distract you from the outside world.

The bar closes at 2 AM, midnight on Sundays.

# ¡CHISPA!

213 WASHINGTON AVENUE
983-6756

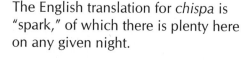

The English translation for *chispa* is "spark," of which there is plenty here on any given night.

This intimate *tapas* bar adjacent to the El Meson Spanish restaurant, is alive with music and dance. The weekly calendar is a mix of flamenco, jazz, world music and Argentine tango (dance invitational). On Tango Night, a bevy of serious dancers are on the floor, and it's very impressive. But since it is "invitational," any brave souls can test their tango skills or sit back and savor the *tapas* served from the full bar.

Open until 11 PM or later, Tuesday through Saturday.

# COWGIRL HALL OF FAME

319 SOUTH GUADALUPE STREET
982-2565

A local favorite for families, couples and on-the-prowl singles.

There's a spacious street-side patio, a raucous bar and a down home restaurant. Live country blues to bluegrass singers/songwriters can be heard throughout the joint.

Old West regalia cover the smoke-free dining room walls, along with archival photos of lady rough riders, trick riders, rodeo queens and honorees inducted into the original Cowgirl Hall of Fame in Fort Worth, Texas.

The menu is all American with a touch of Southwest, e.g. barbecue and grilled meats and fish, New Mexican dishes and Frito pies.

Food is served until midnight, 11 PM on Sunday. The bar closes at 2 AM, midnight on Sunday.

# DEL CHARRO

234 DON GASPAR
954-0326

Neighboring the Inn of the Governors Hotel, this handsome saloon has become one of the most popular gathering places in town.

The full bar features a 41-inch TV for your viewing pleasure, a fireplace is surrounded by soft leather chairs, and the atmosphere is friendly and upbeat.

Perfect for a nightcap, the bar food is delicious and inexpensive featuring homemade potato chips with ranch dressing, quesadillas, nachos, burgers and tostadas ranging in price from four to five bucks. Not bad.

The kitchen stays open 'till midnight.

The bar closes at:
2 AM Friday and Saturday
1 AM Monday through Thursday
Midnight on Sundays

# DIOGENES CLUB

510 GALISTEO STREET
982-1044 / 800-734-7017
www.sfcigar.com

"The Diogenes Club encourages anyone seeking a place outside the noise of popular society to come down for an interesting conversation, a good drink or a fine smoke." So says the proprietor. So there you are, the welcome mat is out at this private club located in the rear of a brick railyard building, circa 1900-1910.

Reminiscent of a cozy English pub, male and female members puff away on full-bodied Nicaraguan, Honduran and Dominican cigars while sipping fine liquors at the full bar, lounge in leather wing chairs and test their skills at the card table or dart board.

If you wish to visit, join ($100 annual dues) or want more information, call or drop by the Santa Fe Cigar Company's main office at 137-D West San Francisco Street.

Enjoy the smoke until 11 PM, Tuesday through Saturday.

# THE DRAGON ROOM

406 OLD SANTA FE TRAIL
983-7712

Adjacent to the famed Pink Adobe Restaurant, this cozy watering hole has been voted "Best Bar" by the local press and one of the Top 19 Bars of the World by *Newsweek International*.

Since its establishment in the 1940s, The Dragon Room's been known as the place where everybody meets everybody in town. The atmosphere is upbeat, featuring kiva fireplaces, trees growing through the roof, colorful tables (painted by the Pink's legendary creator Rosalea Murphy) and an old-time movie theater wagon with on-the-house popcorn.

The nightly menu, served until 9 PM, includes the popular green chile and gypsy stews, sandwiches and fruit 'n' cheese board.

Like locals say, "Meet me at The Pink." Live music three times a week. The bar stays open 'til 1 or 2 AM, midnight on Sunday.

# ELDORADO HOTEL LOUNGE

309 WEST SAN FRANCISCO STREET
988-4455

The lounge is pretty big, but you can find your niche and feel right at home, thanks to plenty of comfortable sofas and club chairs.

Local and guest artists alternate between classic guitar and grand piano seven nights a week. There is no cover charge.

The lounge menu includes pizza, nachos, chicken quesadillas and "the best cheeseburgers in town." The kitchen stays open 'til 11 PM.

The bar closes at 1 AM Friday and Saturday, midnight weekdays.

# EL FAROL

808 CANYON ROAD
983-9912

In 1800, Canyon Road was a dusty trail in need of a saloon. Then in 1835, "La Cantina de Canyon" opened for business and became a popular gathering place and venue for local musicians.

Today the venerable landmark is home to El Farol and is still a favorite destination for musicians, singers, dancers and folks in search of some lively entertainment, a friendly bar and good food.

Live music with R&B, rock 'n' roll, country and salsa keeps the tiny dance floor jammed as the whole place rocks into the wee hours seven nights a week. Classical guitar and flamenco performers take center stage in the "Flamenco Room" on designated evenings.

The dining room and patio offer El Farol's famous *tapas* and a menu of contemporary and traditional Spanish entrees.

The kitchen closes at 10 PM.
The doors close at 2 AM.

# EL PASEO BAR & GRILL

200 GALISTEO STREET
992-2848

Located in the heart of downtown, El Paseo's long and narrow space draws a young crowd that doesn't mind being crowded. Weekends are especially packed when there's live music or a sports event is on the tube. Tuesday is open mic night.

Micro beers are on tap at the full bar. The pub fare includes potato skins, burgers, nachos and chile cheese fries until 10 PM.

A large window opens onto Galisteo Street inviting strollers outside to observe the festivities inside and vice versa.

Windows and doors close at 1:30 AM, midnight Sunday.

# EVANGELO'S

CORNER OF WEST
SAN FRANCISCO &
GALISTEO STREETS
982-9014

Evangelo Klonis, a Greek immigrant and World War II hero, opened this watering hole over sixty years ago. According to Nick, his son and proprietor, Evangelo's is "the only real bar left in Santa Fe."

No food, no comfy club chairs, no host or hostess. Just a big smoky room with bar stools, booths, tables and chairs. A real bar.

The clientele run the gamut from bikers to CEOs. The music is live and eclectic, i.e. blues, rock, jazz, Latin and bluegrass. The dance floor is jammed, and you can hear the din a block away. For those who prefer a quiet game of pool, four tables await you downstairs.

Bring cash. Credit cards and checks are not accepted.

Doors close at 2 AM.

This Evangelo's is located a couple of blocks down the street from the other Evangelo's. It is somewhat akin to a Greek island café where on warm evenings customers sit on a patio under the stars sipping ouzos and gazing at ancient monuments ... except here the view is low riders surfing Galisteo Street.

# EVANGELO'S MEDITERRANEAN CAFÉ

29 GALISTEO STREET
820-6526

Two full bars, one inside, one out, offer over eighty brands of beer and "stiff drinks" for five bucks. Four pool tables, three inside, one out.

Every Friday and Saturday, there's a DJ on board for the dance crowd.

Doors close at 2 AM, midnight on Sunday.

# FOX'S UPSTAIRS BAR & GRILL

720 ST. MICHAELS DRIVE
473-3697

Situated over Kinko's, this neighbor-hood restaurant/sports bar is where, says the owner, "local people come to socialize and eat."

Weather permitting, large windows open to the night air, and a spacious patio overlooks the city lights.

Six TV screens are positioned around the room for sports fans. Live bands for music lovers and karaoke for wannabe crooners.

Friday night is dance night. All holidays, including St. Paddy's and events like Cinco de Mayo, are celebrated throughout the year.

The menu offers burgers, sandwiches and New Mexican dishes until 10 PM Saturday and Sunday.

Open until 2 AM summer, 12:30 AM winter.

Garduño's has a theme. The theme depicts an abandoned margarita factory in old Mexico. If you'd prefer not to eat and drink in a factory, there's a patio just outside the lounge.

# GARDUÑO'S

130 LINCOLN AVENUE (UPSTAIRS)
983-9797

As you down your 17½ ounce "Grande House Margarita," you may want to snack on some guacamole or chile con queso, nachos, quesadillas or oysters on the half shell, as Mariachi bands roam the restaurant each Friday and Saturday evenings.

But wait … there's more. When the clock strikes 9 PM on Wednesdays through Sundays, Garduño's turns into an after hours club, with a mix of Latino nights, hip hop nights, golden oldie nights and Karaoke nights. Late night edibles are available until 12:30 AM.

The bar closes at 1:30 AM. It's *buenas noches* at 2 AM.

# THE GARRETT'S G SPOT

311 OLD SANTA FE TRAIL
946-0561

Adjacent to the Garrett Desert Inn, the G Spot features a full bar, dance space, a big screen TV, two pool tables in an interior of black, grey and stainless steel.

Entertainment alternates between live bands and DJs with an emphasis on Latin music.

The locally famous Father Pretto, better known as the "Salsa Priest," and his band pack the joint every other Friday night.

The eclectic menu lists Asian, New Mexican, Italian and American fare.

A spacious patio facing Old Santa Fe Trail is open in the spring and summer.

Food service ends around 11 PM. The bar closes at 2 AM, midnight on Sundays.

# GREEN ONION

1851 ST. MICHAELS DRIVE
983-5198

The mother of all sports bars is a short drive from downtown. It's the oldest (circa 1970) and is consistently voted the "Best" sports bar in Santa Fe by the local press.

The Onion has a gigantic satellite dish that feeds sports events into twelve TV screens scattered around two rooms.

Between games you can test your skills at foosball, interact with the National Trivia Network and throw darts. (Dart tournaments are held every Tuesday night.)

The booze menu includes drinks with sporting names like "Slam-Dunk," "Triple Play" and "Bad Girl."

Corned beef and cabbage, green chile stew, burgers and New Mexican dishes are served until 9 PM. Pizzas and appetizers 'til 11 PM.

It's all over at 2 AM.

# HOTEL SANTA FE

1501 PASEO DE PERALTA
982-1200

In the mood to drink and dine in a mellow restaurant? You can actually talk in normal tones in the lobby bar of Santa Fe's only Native American owned hotel.

The lodge style interior has plenty of cushy couches and chairs, a full bar, a cornucopia of Indian artifacts and the lilting notes of a wooden flute on Fridays and Saturdays until 9 PM.

In the warm months the adjoining courtyard offers drink and food service, along with the aroma of bread baking in a traditional horno. There is also a large teepee where you might find a storyteller ready to spin a yarn. When the Picuris tribal dancers visit the hotel in authentic headdress and ceremonial attire, you are in for a treat.

The Amaya Restaurant offers a menu with a Native American influence, i.e. bison, quail and venison. I'm sure dishes less "Native" are also available.

Food service 'til 9:30 PM. Bar closes at 10 PM

# LA CASA SENA CANTINA

125 EAST PALACE AVENUE
988-9232

In this far-off Broadway supper club, the charming and talented wait staff sings while dinner is served from the highly touted La Casa Sena menu. Voices hailing from Louisiana, Texas, New York and New Mexico fill the room with Broadway show tunes.

Creative margarita concoctions, vinos from La Casa Sena's award-winning wine cellar and Best of Broadway cocktails with names like "Jekyl & Hyde," "Little Schnapps of Horrors," "Sweeney Todd" and "South Pacific" keep you in the mood for a fun evening.

The show goes on at 5:30 PM and 8 PM. Reservations are recommended.

# LA FONDA FIESTA LOUNGE

100 EAST SAN FRANCISCO
982-5511

The tobacco-free Fiesta Lounge is tucked into a corner of one of Santa Fe's oldest historic hotels. The Lounge attracts hotel guests, tourists and devoted locals who two-step the night away when "honky tonk" country and western music is on tap.

Other evenings you might tune into jazz, Tex Mex, rock 'n' roll or flamenco. There's something for everyone and everyone seems to show up.

La Fonda's menu serves everything from nachos to hamburgers in a friendly, unpretentious atmosphere.

Food service is until 10 PM. The bar closes at 11:30 PM Monday to Thursday, midnight or later Friday and Saturday.

# THE LOBBY BAR

INN AT THE LORETTO
211 OLD SANTA FE TRAIL
988-5531

The living room ambiance makes this a great place to spend an evening with friends. Cozy up to the fireplace, do a little dancing, a little drinking and have a bite to eat from the Loretto's kitchen.

Live music on Friday and Saturday evening with dancing in the summer months. Classical and flamenco guitar on Wednesday and Thursday. Monday night football in the fall and winter.

The bar menu includes quesadillas, shrimp dumplings, buffalo rings, turkey club, etc.

Food service ends at 10 PM. The bar closes at 11 PM or midnight, depending on the crowd.

# LOS MAYAS

409 WEST WATER STREET
986-9930

This family-owned restaurant transports you south of the border with authentic Mexican cuisine and live music seven nights a week.

Musicians and singers perform in the main room and (weather permitting) trellised patio.

Monday and Tuesday it's guitar and vocal, Wednesday it's classical guitar, Thursday accordion and vocal, Friday and Saturday Latin harp, guitar and vocals, and on Sunday it's flamenco guitar and vocal.

The relaxed and friendly atmosphere encourages patrons to join in the festivities by singing along, dancing (i.e. the flamenco) or both.

It's *adios* at 10 PM.

# MARIA'S

555 WEST CORDOVA ROAD
983-7929

Yet another place you can be serenaded by mariachi musicians, but here, the bill of fare is strictly New Mexican.

Maria's has been at the same location for fifty-two years and claims to have written the book on margaritas.

In fact, Maria's margaritas have been voted the "Best in Santa Fe" by the *Santa Fe Reporter* for the last several years. The barkeeps claim to have the wherewithal to concoct up to one hundred variations on this celebrated cocktail.

Mariachis serenade until 10 PM every evening but Monday.

# ORE HOUSE ON THE PLAZA

50 LINCOLN AVENUE AT
SAN FRANCISCO STREET
983-8687

Location. Location. Because the Ore House is smack in the middle of town, it's an easy destination for folks out on a stroll and in need of food and drink.

The balcony overlooking the plaza is great for people watching. Thursday through Sunday musicians keep things lively with blues, jazz, flamenco guitar and bluegrass. There is no dance floor, but "people dance when the music hits them."

Inside you'll find a full bar with plenty of seating, and the bartender promises to switch on the TV for major sports events.

Crab cakes, steak, burgers, quesadillas, seafood, guacamole and all the rest are served until 10 PM summer, 9 PM winter. Closing time is 2 AM.

# PALACE RESTAURANT & SALOON

142 WEST PALACE AVENUE
982-9891

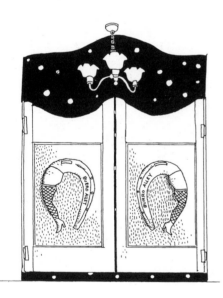

In 1895, Donna Gertrudis Barcelo, known as Miss Trudy, arrived from Mexico and established a gambling saloon adjacent to Burro Alley. The popular watering hole eventually gained the reputation as a house of ill repute, attracting *rico* Santa Feans, French Canadian trappers, American traders and merchants from the East.

In 1959 when the grounds were being excavated for building The Palace Restaurant, a door knocker shaped as half a horseshoe and a woman's leg with the inscription "Burro Alley–1873" was discovered, indicating that Miss Trudy's not only took care of riders but their horses as well.

The present-day saloon maintains much of the flavor of those wild and woolly days with a mahogany bar, red-flocked walls, swinging barroom doors and paintings of femme fatales.

The upscale menu, ranging from neo-Italian Classic to Caesar salad to burgers, is available in the main dining room, courtyard and saloon until 10 PM.

Music varies from piano and guitar, violin to jazz. And it's okay to sing and dance, but please, not on the bar.

Open till late Monday through Saturday. Closed Sunday.

# THE PARAMOUNT

331 SANDOVAL STREET
982-8999

The Paramount is considered the best place in town for dancing, live music, people watching and meeting singles.

Everything is big—the room, the bar, the dance floor and the thunderous sound system, with disco lights pulsing to music performed by nationally known artists on tour, local favorites and prominent DJs when no concerts are scheduled. There's reggae night when the Club Dreads Brotherhood sound system is plugged in and the Rastafarians take to the floor; and salsa on Tuesday night with Mambo Italiano. Most Sunday nights there's mellow country and western with the popular band South by Southwest.

The long bar overlooking the dance floor is a favored meeting place for the young and hip who strain to hear each other over the din.

Because the music menu changes every night of the week, it's advisable to check the club's calendar of events, times and cover.

The bar closes at 2 AM.

# RIO CHAMA BAR

(IN THE RIO CHAMA STEAKHOUSE)
414 OLD SANTA FE TRAIL
955-0765

The Rio Chama Bar is not really a sports bar, and they don't have entertainment, but it deserves mention because it is so comfortable—with low and seductive lighting, cushy armchairs, sofas and upholstered booths.

Rio Chama is popular with politicians during the legislative session and affectionately called "Rio Trauma."

The bar menu specializes in comfort food, e.g. nachos, fried calamari and Angus Burgers. The wine list is impressive and extensive, the full bar boasts a "2 oz. pour" and for sports fans, yes, there is a giant TV tuned to the game, but it's still not a sports bar. It's just a comfy place to watch sports.

Food until 10 PM, open Friday, Saturday and Sunday 'til midnight. The rest of the week doors close at 11 PM.

# ROCKY'S BAR & GRILL

2434 CERRILLOS ROAD
(LOCATED IN COLLEGE
PLAZA SOUTH)
986-1992

Rocky's is one big room, 5,500 square feet to be exact. The space is divided into two sections, one for the six pool tables, the other for dining and boozing.

For sports fans, there's a wall with several TV monitors showing every conceivable athletic event worth showing.

The menu is also large, offering a build-your-own half-pound hamburger, jumbo dogs, pizzas, pastas, French dip sandwiches and steaks.

The kitchen closes at 10 PM. The bar closes at 2 AM.

# RODEO NITES

2911 CERRILLOS ROAD
473-4138

Over the course of an evening, Larry and the Rodeo Boys call out the "Electric Slide," "East Coast Swing," "West Coast Swing," "Cotton-Eye Joe Shuffle" and "Two-Step," as willing hoofers leap onto one of Santa Fe's largest dance floors.

Rodeo Nites is not exclusively Country and Western. Guest performers and DJs come and go with a mix of rock 'n' roll, hip hop and Latin music. Wednesday is Ladies Night, when there's no cover charge and the drinks are cheap (they're pretty cheap anyway.) Thursday is Tequila or New Mexico Night, Friday and Saturday are always Country and Western.

On Sunday, Mexican Night, the cover jumps from the usual $4/$6 to $20. This hefty price tag allows the club to import authentic Mexican bands from El Paso and south of the border.

Doors close at 1:45 AM.

# SECOND STREET BREWERY

1814 SECOND STREET
(OFF CERRILLOS ROAD)
982-3030

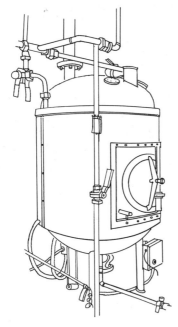

Award-winning handcrafted beers are created on the premises of this friendly neighborhood brewpub. The largely local clientele gather inside the beer hall or choose the trellised patio outside.

Besides nightly music, a slew of special events takes place in the course of the year, e.g. Oktober Fest Release Weekend (when a new lager is introduced), Mardi Gras Crawfish Boil, St. Paddy's Day, and the Brew Master's Dinner with a four-course feast with just the right brew to complement each serving.

The English pub fare includes fish 'n' chips, shepherd's pie and London broil. Wine is available.

Open until 1 AM weekends, midnight on week nights.

# SILVA LANES

1325 RUFINA CIRCLE
471-2110

After bowling down pins on one of the Silva's thirty-two lanes, game lovers can choose a variety of distractions.

To the right is a large room where you can test your skill at pool, video games and air hockey.

To the left is a smoke-filled lounge (known as "Punky's Place) with TVs, pool tables and "Punky's Karaoke Machine." The karaoke host keeps things lively six nights a week by encouraging guests to cheer singers on as they wander the floor armed with a cordless microphone.

If all this activity stimulates your appetite, there's a snack bar serving hot dogs, tacos, Frito pies, etc.

The balls keep rolling until 2 AM Friday and Saturday, midnight Sunday through Thursday.

# THE STAAB HOUSE LOUNGE

(AT LA POSADA DE SANTA FE
RESORT AND SPA)
330 EAST PALACE AVENUE
986-0000

In 1882, an Easterner named Abraham Staab built a stately Victorian mansion for his young bride Julie.

Julie loved to show off her new home and entertained endlessly, so the Staab house soon became a favorite hangout for Santa Fe society.

Much time has passed, but the party goes on in the very rooms where Julie held court. The cherry wood bar and salon, the Rose Room and library are popular gathering places for locals and visitors. In the small sitting room off the library one can enjoy a cigar.

The bar menu offers contemporary Southwest cuisine that includes Staab House nachos and an impressive list from the wine cellar.

The lounge features live music ranging from jazz to flamenco.

Word has it that Julie's ghost has been sighted many times as she wanders her beloved home. Not long ago a shocked security guard saw her descending the grand staircase.

So drink up and keep a watchful eye until 1 AM Friday and Saturday, midnight Sunday through Thursday.

# SWIG

135 WEST PALACE AVENUE,
THIRD FLOOR
955-0400

This stylish night spot is comprised of four lounges, each with its own bar, comfortable seating and a delectable appetizer menu.

Swig's bartenders offer a list of innovative "specialty cocktails," including variations on the sacred martini. A daring undertaking to say the least.

Executive chef Eric Distefano's "Asian tapas" and scrumptious deserts are reason enough to visit this Trendy club.

Each lounge is named by a color. Three (white, orange and blue) share the same sensual music and serene ambiance, while one flight down, the Red Room features live performers, DJs and a dance floor with male and female GoGo dancers. What more could you ask for?

Dress is fashionably casual. Smoking in the Orange Lounge only.

Food is served until 11 PM. Doors open from 5 PM "till later" Friday and Saturday, 5 PM to midnight Tuesday through Thursday.

This cozy French bistro was named "Restaurant of the Year" by the *Santa Fe Reporter's* 2002-03 "Guide to Dining" publication—and deservedly so.

# 315 RESTAURANT & WINE BAR

315 OLD SANTA FE TRAIL
986-9190
www.315santafe.com

315's chef and owner Louis Moskow's enthusiasm for creating delicious meals is matched only by his passion for the grape, thus the Wine Bar.

Moskow enjoys playing host to connoisseurs and novices alike. His list of wines numbers 200, with forty wines by the glass.

A wine-friendly menu includes delicacies such as basil wrapped shrimp with apricot chutney and curry sauce.

Scrutinize, swirl, sniff and sip until 10 PM. Open seven nights a week.

# TINY'S

1015 PEN ROAD
(SOUTHEAST CORNER
OF ST. FRANCIS DRIVE
& CERRILLOS ROAD)
983-9817

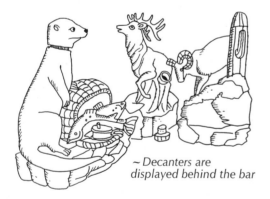

*~ Decanters are
displayed behind the bar*

This unpretentious Santa Fe landmark has plenty of parking and local color. Patrons cut loose and dance the night away to local bands playing R&B, country and western, rock 'n' roll and golden oldies. The party takes place both in the '50s style lounge and out on the patio.

A large authentic New Mexican menu, plus steaks, seafood, salads, etc., is served until 10 PM.

And for what it's worth, "the Southwest's largest decanter collection" of Jim Beam, Ezra Brooks, Ski Country, Wild Turkey and Lionstone is displayed behind the bar.

Live music ends at 12-12:30 AM. Doors close at 1 AM.

# VANESSIE

A CONTINENTAL-AMERICAN
STEAKHOUSE
434 WEST SAN FRANCISCO
982-9966

Treat yourself to an evening at this upscale restaurant/piano bar, and you'll be happy you did. The attentive staff serves Texas-size servings from an à la carte menu that includes New Zealand rack of lamb, ribs, chicken Caesar and a juicy hamburger.

In the lounge you'll find a full bar and all your favorite songs and show tunes for a singalong. Two talented performers, Doug Montgomery and Charles Tichenor, alternate evenings at the concert grand piano. It's very entertaining and a regular hangout for locals.

Dinner service ends at 9:30 PM winter, 10:30 PM summer. The bar and music keep going 'til 11 PM or midnight or later, "depending on the crowd."

AFTER HOURS means after
10 PM in Santa Fe. The following
establishments keep the kitchen
open until midnight or after.

# AFTER HOURS DINING

# THE ARTIST PUB

(ST. FRANCIS HOTEL)
210 DON GASPAR AVENUE
983-5700

The Artist Pub is located off the lobby in the St. Francis Hotel.
Reminiscent of an English pub, the tabletops are marble and the
bar top is copper. Above the fireplace and dark walnut paneling
is a large fresco (hence the name "Artist Pub").

The menu includes grilled sea scallops, braised pork tostadas,
grilled hanger steak and the St. Francis burger.

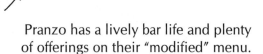

# PRANZO
# ITALIAN
# GRILL

540 MONTEZUMA
984-2645

Pranzo has a lively bar life and plenty
of offerings on their "modified" menu.

Choices include pizzas (margarita, calzone,
molto carne, etc.) antipastos (carpaccio, calamari, etc.)
salads (Caesar, insalata mista, etc.) and a homemade soup.

The influx of **Casinos** to New Mexico has brought with it another way to spend an evening ... or a night.

CASINOS

# CAMEL ROCK CASINO

TESUQUE PUEBLO
800-462-2635 / 800-GO CAMEL

About ten miles north of town on U.S. 285, you'll come upon two camels. On the left, a rock formation resembling a camel. On the right is a casino named after the camel on the left. Owned and operated by the Tesuque Pueblo, Camel Rock Casino offers everything from slots, roulette, craps, black jack and video poker to bingo. Entertainment varies from live music to stand-up comedians, and the café provides an all-you-can-eat buffet. This casino is alcohol free.

# CITIES OF GOLD CASINO & SPORTS BAR

POJOAQUE PUEBLO
455-3313 / 800-455-3313

The Pojoaque Pueblo, a few miles north of the camel, is home to the Cities of Gold Casino. Gamblers here are offered the gamut of games in addition to live entertainment and food. The adjacent Golden Cantina Lounge provides booze and simulcast horse and greyhound racing. A free shuttle makes several pickups from Santa Fe. The Casino is open 24 hours Friday and Saturday. Doors close 4 AM Sunday through Thursday.

# CASINO HOLLYWOOD

SAN FELIPE PUEBLO
867-6700

South of town on the way to Albuquerque is where you'll find Casino Hollywood. In addition to a fully loaded gambling establishment (with no booze), there is a sport and concert arena, as well as a 24-hour gas station and convenience store.

Open 24 hours Thursday through Saturday. Doors close 4 AM Sunday through Wednesday.

ODDS AND ENDS

# LONGEVITY CAFÉ & EMPORIUM

PLAZA MERCADO AT
WATER AND GALISTEO
986-0403
www.longevitycafe.com

There is abundant nightlife in downtown Santa Fe, but is it good for you? There is one place that is concerned about your health and well-being: the Longevity Café, "your downtown oasis."

It's all very Zen with organic teas and coffees, "Longevity Pies" and assorted healthy snacks.

The specialties of the house are the tasty "Power Shakes" that include: the "Power Plant" for instant energy; the "Chi Devil," a tonic designed to turnon a woman's sexuality; the "Mighty Joe Young," a virility tonic for men; plus drinks that "kill the flu" and "banish the blues."

The atmosphere is friendly and comfortable with room to roam about as you check out the selection of health-giving products, books, magazines, gifts and artwork.

You can work on a long, healthy life until midnight Monday to Saturday, 7 PM Sunday.

# ODD FELLOWS AND REBEKAHS

1125 CERRILLOS ROAD
983-7493

When was the last time you went to a barn dance or spent an evening devoted to Scottish country dancing? Chances are, the answer is "not lately"—or "never."

Opportunity awaits at Odd Fellows Hall, and don't be shy—novices are welcome and the place couldn't be friendlier. Israeli dancing, square dancing, international folk dancing, salsa and swing are regularly available.

You can easily miss this modest little building, so keep your eyes peeled between Cordova and Baca Street on Cerrillos Road. There's no neon, so the porch light is the only sign it's open.

Scottish dance is on Friday, International Folk on Tuesday, Israeli on Sunday. It's best to check the schedule posted on the front of the building.

# R&B

709 DON CUBERO
(ACROSS FROM THE TRAVEL
LODGE ON CERRILLOS)
992-8002

R&B stands for both Ribs
& Burgers and Rhythm & Blues.

The restaurant is a house that is
a restaurant. The dining room was
once a living room. An adjacent
parlor, also for dining, features
live music nightly.

The backyard is filled with benches,
tables and an enormous smoker that
prepares your ribs nice and slow in
apple wood.

All meals, including Cornish hen
and smoked shrimp, come with
coleslaw, beans, potatoes, corn
on the cob, peppers and a tortilla.

All meals are served in Styrofoam
containers with compartments for
each food item. Why? "No dishwasher
helps keep the prices low." (Dinners
range from $6.95 to $8.95.)

Look for the yellow bear next to the
house that is a restaurant.

The kitchen closes at 9 PM.

# ROCKIN' ROLLER EVENT ARENA

22915 AGUA FRIA
473-7755

For years, parents have booked this place for their kids' birthday parties. It has a spacious floor for roller skating, dancing or whatever, a DJ who keeps everybody rockin' and rollin', a snack bar, a video arcade, karaoke and management who will work with you to make every party a success.

The Arena is not exclusively for little kids and birthdays, it's also for big people. It's an event arena. So think up an event. Throw a party.

Call to reserve and confirm.

# TEN THOUSAND WAVES

3.5 MILES UP
HYDE PARK ROAD
982-9304

Need a little pampering? This soothing Japanese health spa combines the "ancient Japanese traditions of healing and relaxation."

Rejuvenation takes place in communal or private hot tubs, cold plunges, full-service massages, foot treatments, facials ... you name it. Kimonos, towels, hair dryers, etc., are provided, and healthy snacks and beverages are available.

You can continue to unwind by staying the night in one of the resort's luxury lodgings.

Indulge until midnight on Friday and Saturday, 10:30 PM weeknights.

# WAREHOUSE 21

1614 PASEO DE PERALTA
989-4423
www.warehouse21.org

Warehouse 21 is Santa Fe's nationally acclaimed center for teens and young adults, ages 12–21. An average of 400 workshops and 100 special events take place each year.

The 3,500 square foot facility features offices, performance space, darkroom lab, recording studio, silkscreen studio and a "hangout" internet room.

Due to its growing popularity and need for more elbow room, a new facility three times the present size is on the drawing board.

Evenings are stimulating, fun and always entertaining. Live concerts with local youth bands, open mic poetry, comedy shows, performance art, DJs, movies and much more take place in this hassle-free space where kids relax and chill out.

W21 has strict, no-nonsense rules regarding drugs, alcohol and rowdy behavior.

SPECIAL INTEREST INDEX

## AFTER HOURS

Atomic Grill
Back Road Pizza
Bar B
Casinos (3)
Catamount
Cheeks
¡Chispa!
Cowgirl
Dragon Room
El Farol
El Paseo
Evangelo's
Fox's Upstairs
Garduño's
Garrett's G Spot
Green Onion
Palace
Paramount
Radisson Cabaret Room
Rodeo Nites
Second Street Brewery
Silva Lanes
Swig
Tiny's

## DANCING

Catamount
¡Chispa!
El Farol
Evangelo's
Evangelo's Mediterranean
Fox's Upstairs
Garduño's
Garrett's G Spot
La Fonda's Fiesta Lounge
Odd Fellows Hall
Paramount
Rodeo Nites
Swig—Red Room
Tiny's

## POOL TABLES

Back Road Pizza
Cheeks
Catamount
Evangelo's
Evangelo's Mediterranean
Garrett's G Spot
Rocky's
Silva Lanes
Swig

## SINGLE SCENE

Atomic Grill
Back Road Pizza
Bar B
Catamount
Cowgirl
Dragon Room
El Farol
El Paseo
Fox's Upstairs
Garrett's G Spot
La Fonda Fiesta Lounge
Oasis Café
Odd Fellows Hall
Ore House
Paramount
Second Street Brewery
Swig

## SPORTS BARS

Blue Corn Café
Catamount
Cities of Gold Sports Bar
Fox's Upstairs
Green Onion
Rocky's
Silva Lanes

## LIVE ENTERTAINMENT

Atomic Grill
Back Road Pizza
Bar B
Maria Benitez Cabaret Room
Catamount
Cheeks
¡Chispa!
Cowgirl
Dragon Room
El Farol
El Paseo
Evangelo's
Fox's Upstairs
Garduño's
Garrett's G Spot
La Casa Sena Cantina
Los Mayas
Inn at Loretto
Ore House
Palace
Paramount
Rodeo Nites
Second Street Brewery
Staab House Bar
Swig
Tiny's
Vanessie

Santa Fe is brimming with cultural events
most every night of the year.

To stay up-to-date with the week's attractions, check
with the local press. (Details are in the Introduction.)
Another source is on the web. Every Friday the
Santa Fe Convention & Visitors Bureau (CVB)
publishes a *Culture, Arts & Tourism Calendar,*
which is emailed to hotels, galleries, organizations
and individuals. It can also be downloaded from
CVB's website at *Santa Fe.org.*

For future performing arts events, pick up an issue of
*4 Seasons of Performances.* Published twice a year
(June and September), this publication has a calendar
guide for all the four seasons.

I found my copy in the lobby of the Lensic.

# CULTURE AFTER DARK

THEATER

# LENSIC
## Performing Arts Center

211 WEST SAN FRANCISCO STREET
988-1234
www.lensic.com

When the Lensic Theater first opened in 1931, it was a vaudeville and motion picture house with a ballroom, café, soda fountain, men's club and confectionary. A visiting journalist described it as "the most splendid theater in the west."

Because of a recent $8.5 million renovation, the Lensic has been restored to its former glory.

This year-round performing arts center features local, national and international artists who fill the programming calendar with music, dance, plays, musicals, films, readings and community events. The Lensic is undeniably the Jewel of Santa Fe.

# SANTA FE PERFORMING ARTS COMPANY & SCHOOL

ARMORY FOR THE ARTS THEATER
1050 OLD PECOS TRAIL
982-7992

According to the *Santa Fe Reporter*, the community voted Performing Arts the "Best Local Theater Group."

Performing Arts produces nine lively shows a year:  three adult, three young people (8-12 years) and three teenage performances.

Says the company's artistic director, Wayne Sabato, "We give local artists an opportunity to work on wonderful material from new plays to tried and trues to musicals."

Performing Arts is also a venue for outside companies.

# THEATERWORK

1336 RUFINA CIRCLE
471-1799
www.theaterwork.org

Theaterwork is a year-round professional company housed in a large industrial building on the town's south side.

Artistic Director David Olson and his ensemble consistently deliver some of Santa Fe's best productions of classic and original works.

Most Theaterwork productions are sold out every season, so make your reservations early.

# SANTA FE PLAY-HOUSE

142 EAST DEVARGAS STREET
988-4262

Founded in 1922, the Santa Fe Playhouse is the oldest
continuously running theater company west of the Mississippi
and is located in one of America's oldest neighborhoods.

So much for old. The Playhouse delivers fresh, new innovative
productions year round, guided by local directors who stage musicals,
comedies, dramas, murder mysteries and classics.

# JAMES A. LITTLE THEATER

NEW MEXICO SCHOOL FOR THE DEAF CAMPUS
1060 CERRILLOS ROAD
476-6497

This is one of the more eclectic venues in town.
Dance, music, theater and community gatherings share this
stage year round. The theater seats 300, and there is plenty of parking.

# GREER GARSON THEATER

COLLEGE OF SANTA FE
1600 ST. MICHAELS DRIVE
473-6511, www.cfs.educ

Named in honor of the "First Lady" of stage and screen, the Greer Garson Theater stages four major performances a year, ranging from dramas to comedy to musicals. This comfortable theater seats 500.

The nationally recognized College of Santa Fe Performing Arts Department operates the theater, where shows are performed by college students and are often directed by faculty members.

# PANDEMONIUM PRODUCTIONS

VENUE: JAMES A. LITTLE THEATER
920-0704
www.pand.prod@aol

Pandemonium is a children's theater company consisting of thirty to forty young people ranging in age from eight to eighteen. The year's season is comprised of three performances – two musicals and one comedy.

# SANTA FE STAGES

422 WEST SAN FRANCISCO STREET
982-6680
www.santafestages.org

Santa Fe Stages brings nationally
and internationally acclaimed
performances to town via New York,
Los Angeles and London, as well
as providing showcases for local
Santa Fe artists.

Check the web for updated
information.

# THEATER GROTTESCO

VARIOUS VENUES
474-8400
www.theatergrottesco.org
grottesco@earthlink.net

Artistic Director John Flax, the
co-founder of Theater Grottesco,
moved his French formed touring
company to North American in
the 1980s and settled in The City
Different in 1996.

The internationally acclaimed
ensemble has performed in seven
countries, thirty states, hundreds of
communities and major U.S. cities.

Performed without words, this wholly original
theater is "joyous," "smart," "funny" and truly
eloquent with "vigorous physicality and visual
imagery." The Italian word *grottesco* means
larger than life, not grotesque.

Grottesco plays only once a year, so you'd
better plan to be in town between May and
June if you want to catch the show.

MUSIC

# SANTA FE OPERA

7 MILES NORTH OF TOWN
ON U.S. 84/285
800-280-4654
www.santafeopera.org

"One of the most breathtakingly beautiful venues for opera it is possible to imagine." *The London Telegraph*

Perched atop a mesa overlooking the Jemez and Sangre de Cristo Mountains, this unique theater, open on both sides, affords panoramic views, dramatic sunsets and evening breezes.

The Opera is universally recognized for the quality of its productions and variety of its repertory. Celebrated voices from the U.S. and abroad take the stage late June to the end of August.

Every seat has a screen with instantaneous translation so you won't miss a thing in any language. Pre-show arrivals may purchase a "sumptuous" buffet supper and there is a free introductory talk on the opera you are about to enjoy. Or, do as many do, bring your own festive dinner for a tailgate party in the parking lot.

It is recommended that you bring a jacket, as summer breezes often turn cool after dark.

As much a "visionary as an architect,"
Soleri developed his own "organically
expressive" architectural style after
apprenticing to Frank Lloyd Wright.

# PAOLO SOLERI AMPHITHEATER

SANTA FE INDIAN SCHOOL CAMPUS
1501 CERRILLOS ROAD
989-6320
www.ticketmaster.com

Ten times each summer, a sell-out crowd
fills the 2,900 seat open-air theater as an
impressive line-up of big and almost big
name performers take the stage.

Among other glitterati, artists have
included Kenny G, BB King, Ziggy
Marley, Bob Dylan, James Taylor, KD
Lang, Santana and Gordon Lightfoot.
Depending on the featured artist, you
must move early for tickets or end up
standing, or worse, not even.

# SANTA FE COMMUNITY ORCHESTRA

ST. FRANCIS AUDITORIUM
107 WEST PALACE AVENUE
473-2688
www.sfco.org

This twenty-year-old orchestra finds musician members among all walks of our community. Doctors, teachers, students, scientists, retirees, homemakers, etc., all sharing a love of music and dedication to their instruments come together to make this orchestra happen.

The conductor is a professional, and at various times during the year well-known guest artists join the orchestra. A six-concert series includes something for everyone from Mozart to Strauss to Debussy to homegrown composers.

# MUSIC ONE
## The Santa Fe Concert Association

VENUES:
LENSIC THEATER
& ST. FRANCIS AUDITORIUM

In its 67th season, the Association presents a repertoire with a range of music from historical to the 20th century, as performed by internationally recognized artists and ensembles.

# SANTA FE PRO MUSICA

~ Loretto Chapel

The 35-member Santa Fe Chamber Orchestra specializes in music of the 17th and 18th centuries. Often, the group performs without a conductor in order to establish the spontaneous quality of the music that was typical of that period.

World-renowned artist guest appearances make each season a special one.

As an affiliate of the Smithsonian Institution, Pro Musica performs on historic instruments in its Chamber Ensemble series, featuring programs of Mozart, Haydn, Krommer and Bach. Santa Fe's Bach Festival and popular Baroque Christmas Concerts take place in the intimate Loretto Chapel.

The season opens in September and concludes with the Spring Serenade in May.

# SANTA FE CHAMBER MUSIC FESTIVAL

VENUES: ST. FRANCIS
AUDITORIUM &
THE LENSIC
& SITE SANTA FE
983-2075 OR
982-1890
www.santafe
chambermusic.org

~St. Francis
Auditorium

World-class musicians draw large, enthusiastic crowds as the
Santa Fe Chamber Music Festival celebrates the art of
chamber music each spring and summer.

Events include Bach and Mozart to living composers-in-residence
with concerts spanning four centuries of classical music to jazz.

# SANTA FE SYMPHONY & CHORUS

AT THE LENSIC
983-3530 OR 983-1414
www.sf-symphony.org

Santa Fe's full symphony and chorus
performs concerts and festivals
annually from October through May.

The professional members are all
New Mexico musicians with a wide
range of national and international
experience.

The Chorus comprises
singers from throughout
Northern New Mexico.

# SANGRE DE CRISTO CHORALE

VENUES: SANTA MARIA
DE LA PAZ CATHOLIC
CHURCH, ELDORADO HOTEL
& SANTUARIO DE GUADALUPE
662-5445
www.sdc-choral.org

The Sangre de Cristo Chorale
is an ensemble that has provided
music and voice to Northern New
Mexico communities for over
twenty-five years.

From Christmas to late spring,
the 35-member chorus performs
Baroque Choral, international folk
music and contemporary works.

# SANTA FE DESERT CHORALE

VENUES INCLUDE:
LORETTO CHAPEL,
SANTUARIO DE GUADALUPE,
THE LENSIC & CRISTO REY
CHURCH ON UPPER
CANYON ROAD
988-2282
www.desertchorale.org

~Santuario de Guadalope

The Santa Fe Desert Chorale is a fully professional
twenty-voice ensemble whose members hail from
twelve states, ranging from New York to California.

The summer festival offers 15 concerts in 5 repertoires,
plus several special community events.

The winter holiday season begins Christmas week and
continues through the following week. The Chorus performs
mostly a cappella with works representing nine centuries
of music from ancient to modern.

# SANTA FE WOMEN'S ENSEMBLE

VENUES:
LORETTO CHAPEL
& SANTUARIO DE
GUADALUPE
954-4922
www.sfwe.org

Santa Fe's unique thirteen-voice choir performs music from the Middle Ages to contemporary commissioned pieces.

The ensemble has been performing to enthusiastic audiences for twenty-three seasons. There are two concerts during the year, one in December at Loretto Chapel and the spring offering at Santuario de Guadalupe.

The long list of national and international companies that dance into town hail from New York and Chicago to St. Petersburg and Senegal.

Then there's Santa Fe's very own dancers and dance companies, such as Aspen Santa Fe Ballet, Maria Benitez Teatro Flamenco, Moving People Dance Company and Cathy Roe Productions.

DANCE

# ASPEN SANTA FE BALLET

VENUE: LENSIC
PERFORMING ARTS CENTER
www.aspensantafeballet.com

This ballet company is comprised of eleven classically trained dancers.

The troop performs an eclectic repertoire of universally recognized choreographers.

# CATHY ROE PRODUCTIONS

VENUE:
JAMES A. LITTLE THEATER
474-4045
www.cathyroe.com

Cathy Roe is a pre-professional dance company consisting of thirty girls, ages thirteen to twenty-two.

There are two shows a year. The holiday performances are just about always on Thanksgiving weekend, while the spring concert is in the last weeks of May. Both shows are usually sellouts.

# FLAMENCO

Lovers of flamenco are kept happy
in Santa Fe. Venues for this fiery
Latin dance flare up all over town.

**El Farol**, for instance, has a
special "Flamenco Room." **¡Chispa!**
at El Meson has flamenco shows every week, and visiting dancers
and dance troupes take the stage at local theaters all through
the year. Sometimes it's a spontaneous performance by someone
or several someones who can't control their passion for the dance.
It's everywhere.

Two months a year the spotlight is on the legendary Maria Benitez
and her internationally renowned **Maria Benitez Teatro Flamenco**.
Ms. Benitez is joined by premier Spanish dancers, musicians and
singers for a show you don't want to miss. Teatro Flamenco
performs late June to early September at the Radisson Hotel,
750 North St. Francis Drive. For tickets, call 888-435-2636.

# MOVING PEOPLE DANCE THEATER

VENUE: JAMES A. LITTLE THEATER
438-9180

This contemporary dance company performs
each spring, summer and winter, bringing a
broad spectrum of dance, including ballet,
jazz and modern.

# NEW MEXICO DANCE COALITION

820-2636
www.nmdancecoalition.org

The Dance Coalition represents New Mexican
dancers and dance companies and is a reliable
source for information concerning dance-related
comings and goings in Santa Fe.

# RAILYARD PERFORMANCE CENTER

1611 PASEO
DE PERALTA
982-8309

The Railyard Center
is a venue for yoga
classes, community
events, social dances,
movement art and a
showcase for local,
national and international
dancers and musicians.

# PERFORMING ARTS: DIRECTORY & MAP

**(1) St. Francis Auditorium**
The auditorium is located inside the Museum of Fine Art, 107 East Palace Avenue.

**(2) Lensic Performing Arts Center**
Downtown at 211 West San Francisco Street

**(3) Loretto Chapel**
211 Old Santa Fe Trail (next to the Inn at Loretto).

**(4) Santa Fe Playhouse**
Located three blocks from the Plaza at 142 East DeVargas Street in the Barrio de Ancino.

**(5) Santa Fe Performing Arts Company**
The Armory for the Arts Theater, 1050 Old Pecos Trail.

**(6) James A. Little Theater**
Located on the New Mexico School for the Deaf campus. The entrance is on Cerrillos just south of St. Francis Drive.

**(7) Theaterworks**
Drive south from town on Cerrillos Road, go past Siler Road and turn right on Calle del Cielo. Go straight—you'll end up on Rufina Circle and at the theater.

**(8) Greer Garson Theater**
Located on the College of Santa Fe campus. Enter at 1600 St. Michaels Drive and follow the signs.

**(9) Paolo Soleri Amphitheater**
Enter the Santa Fe Indian School campus from 1501 Cerrillos Road and follow directions.

**(10) SITE Santa Fe**
1606 Paseo de Peralta, on the corner of Paseo de Peralta and Cerrillos Road. You can't miss it.

**(11) Railyard Performance Center**
1611 Paseo de Peralta. Follow the tracks.

**(12) Santuario de Guadalupe**
100 South Guadalupe, between Alameda and Agua Fria Streets.

**(13) Radisson Hotel**
750 North St. Francis Drive.

**(14) Santa Fe Opera**
7 miles north of town on US 84/285.

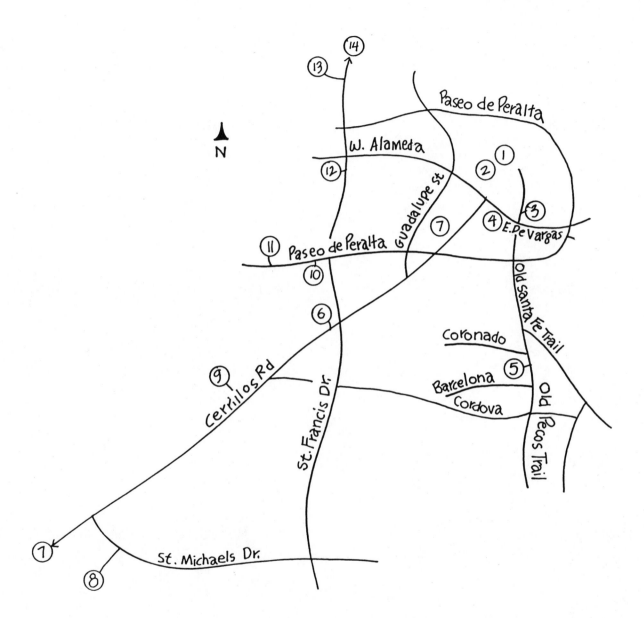

N

14

13

Paseo de Peralta

W. Alameda

12

Guadalupe st

2  1

Paseo de Peralta

11

10

7

4  E. De Vargas

3

Old Santa Fe Trail

6

Coronado

5

Cerrillos Rd

9

Barcelona

Cordova

St. Francis Dr.

Old Pecos Trail

7

St. Michaels Dr.

8

CINEMA

# JEAN COCTEAU CINEMA

418 MONTEZUMA AVENUE
BETWEEN THE RAILROAD
& SANBUSCO CENTER
988-2711

The centrally located Jean Cocteau
is within walking distance from the
Plaza and many of Santa Fe's finest
restaurants. An intimate "art" theater,
it shows independent and foreign films, as well as "sleeper" hits.

In addition to unusual movie snacks, the concession stand offers
fresh brewed coffee, tea and a selection of delicious popcorn toppings.

A unique feature is the VIP screening room with comfortable seating
for four. Movie fans can reserve this cozy theater within a theater for
an additional $3.25 per ticket. Benefits include a sound system you
can control, a soundproof room in which you can laugh, cry and
converse in full voice. Just like home.

# CCA CINEMATHEQUE

1050 OLD SANTA FE TRAIL
982-1338

CCA Cinematheque offers domestic and foreign films that are unlikely to find their way into mainstream movie houses.

CCA also hosts a variety of live performances, lectures, poetry readings, music programs and exhibitions.

For a weekly schedule of events, check the local newspaper—or better yet, lay your hands on CCA's calendar publication found at the CCA or Lensic lobby.

# THE SCREEN

COLLEGE OF SANTA FE CAMPUS
1600 ST. MICHAELS DRIVE
473-6494

The Screen's screen is curved. The Screen's sound system is Dolby. The Screen's projection system is state of the art. And, for our viewing pleasure, the theater has (semi) stadium seating. It's all very civilized and up to date.

Brent Kleiwer is a member of the college faculty and director of film programming for The Screen.

Since Mr. Kleiwer chooses the programs and is a film buff/historian with an infinite knowledge of the cinema, he often enlightens the audience by speaking about the film before it's shown.

The Screen features first-run Art and Independent films, combined with a mix of repertory and archival titles.

They even have popcorn.

# ST. JOHNS COLLEGE

PETERSON STUDENT CENTER
1160 CAMINO CRUZ BLANCA
984-6139 OR 984-6104

The choices of films here are made by students but not the same students every time, resulting in a mixed bag of foreign, documentary, independent, silent classics, etc.

Because there is no publicity for this program, you need to find out the whats and whens by calling for information and a catalog.

# UNITED ARTIST CINEMAS

Santa Fe's mainstream United Artist theaters are located
in two shopping malls. Both provide six screens
in each of the three theaters.

Villa Linda Mall has two multi-screen cinemas.
UA North plays big budget and first-run films.
UA South caters to families, teens and car chase fans.

DeVargas Mall has its share of mainstream movies but manages to add foreign,
independent and sleeper hits to its roster.

VILLA LINDA MALL
4250 CERRILLOS ROAD
NORTH: 471-3377
SOUTH: 471-6066

DEVARGAS MALL
564 NORTH GUADALUPE STREET
988-2773

# DREAM CATCHER CINEMA

753-0887

Another option is in Española, a twenty-minute drive
north of town. This new state-of-the-arts theater has
six screens, stadium seating and digital sound.
The movies are mainstream.

# CINEMA: DIRECTORY & MAP

Santa Fe's eclectic roster of one-screen and six-screen theaters is located in and around the city's nooks and crannies, schools and malls.

## (1) Villa Linda Mall
At the intersection of Rodeo Road and Cerrillos Road. The UA theaters are located on the north and south sides of the mall.

## (2) College of Santa Fe and "Screen" Theater
The College entrance is easy to find, but you'll have to keep a sharp eye for the "Screen" signs; they're small, but they're there.

## (3) St. John's College
Once you're on the campus, it would be best to find a student and ask for directions to the Peterson Student Center.

## (4) Plan B CCA
Turn off Old Pecos Trail into the Armory of the Arts Theater parking area and continue down the (dirt) road to the next parking lot, and you will have arrived.

## (5) Jean Cocteau Cinema
Located on Montezuma Street, between Guadalupe Street and the Sanbusco Market Center.

## (6) Lensic Performing Arts Center
Downtown on San Francisco Street.

## (7) DeVargas Cinema
Enter the DeVargas Mall from Guadalupe Street.

## (8) Dream Catcher
Go north on US 285 and look for the theaters just south of Española.

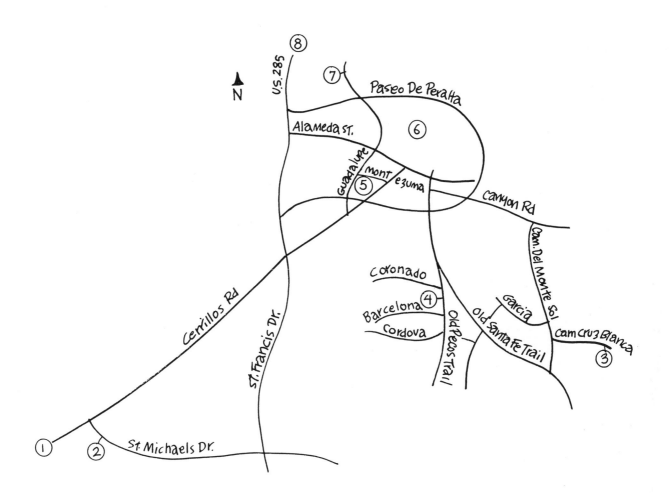

N

U.S. 285

⑧

⑦

Paseo De Peralta

Alameda St.

⑥

Guadalupe

montezuma

⑤

Canyon Rd

Cam. Del Monte Sol

Cerrillos Rd

St. Francis Dr.

Coronado

Barcelona ④

Garcia

Cordova

Old Pecos Trail

Old Santa Fe Trail

Cam Cruz Blanca

③

①

②

St. Michaels Dr.